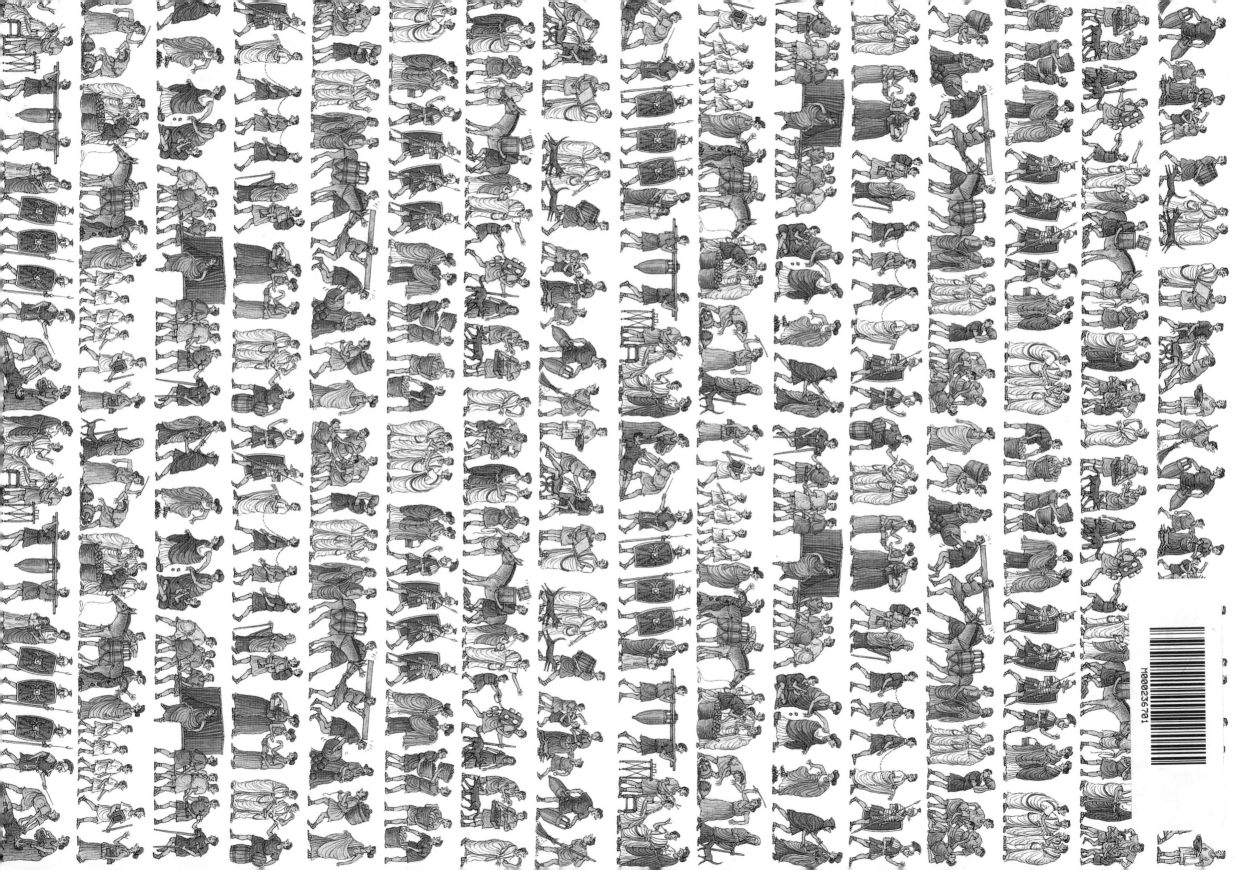

ROME

STEPHEN BIESTY

In Spectacular Cross-Section

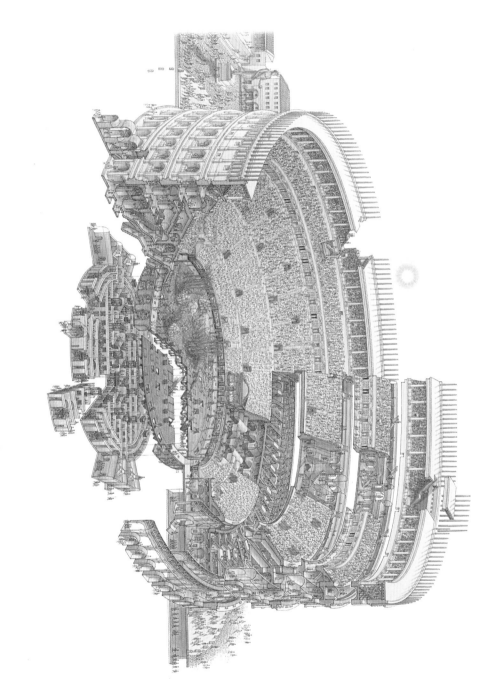

Text by Andrew Solway

Consultant: James Morwood (Wadham College, Oxford)

SCHOLASTIC NONFICTION

Oxford University Press
Great Clarendon Street, Oxford, England OX2 6DP

Library of Congress Cataloging-in-Publication Data
Solway, Andrew.
Rome: in spectacular cross-section / written by Andrew Solway; illustrations by Stephen Biesty.
p. cm.
Includes index.
Summary: Detailed illustrations with explanatory captions and narrative text survey some sites in ancient Rome, including the house of a wealthy family, the Colosseum, the Baths of Trajan, and the Temple of Jupiter.
1. Rome—Social life and customs—Juvenile literature. 2. Rome—Civilization—Juvenile literature. [1. Rome—Social life and customs. 2. Rome—Civilization.] I. Biesty, Stephen, ill. II. Title.

DG78 .S68 2003
937—dc21   2002070694

0-439-45546-4

10 9 8 7 6 5 4 3 2 1   03 04 05 06 07

Printed in Italy
First printing, April 2003

A Note on B.C./A.D. Abbreviations

Throughout this book, you will see that dates appear with the abbreviations "A.D." and "B.C." These terms are used to keep track of years in the Gregorian calendar, which is the one commonly used today. In the Gregorian calendar, years are counted from the year in which Jesus Christ was thought to have been born. Any year after this is written with the letters A.D. before it (for example, A.D. 2003). "A.D." stands for the Latin words "Anno Domini," which mean "in the year of the Lord." Years before the birth of Jesus Christ are counted backward and have the letters B.C. after them (for example, 55 B.C). "B.C." stands for "before Christ." Sometimes people choose to use the abbreviations B.C.E (meaning "Before the Common Era" or "Before the Christian Era") and C.E. (meaning "Common Era" or "Christian Era") instead of B.C. and A.D.

Contents

Titus Cotta and Marcus Cotta Maximus

Titus Cotta is the son of an important Roman senator named Marcus Cotta Maximus. They live in an elegant house on Viminal Hill, not far from the center of Rome. Titus doesn't go to school; he has lessons with his own tutor. But today is a festival day, so there are no lessons. Titus and his father have a busy day planned.

Rome, A.D. 128

This is the city of Rome in the year A.D. 128. It's the biggest city in the ancient world — more than a million people live here. And it's at the center of a huge empire stretching all the way from Egypt to Britain.

Today is the festival of the twin gods Castor and Pollux. There's a parade this morning, so people are making an early start. One of them is Titus Cotta Maximus. His father, Marcus, has promised to take him to the Colosseum and to the chariot races.

Forum of Trajan
Emperor Trajan built this magnificent forum and shopping complex. Trajan was emperor before Hadrian. Titus doesn't remember him, but his father does.

Forum Romanum
The Forum was once a market square; now it's the center of Rome. The most powerful magistrates and politicians in Rome (the senators) meet at the Senate House (the Curia). The most important courts of law are held in the Basilica Julia and the Basilica Aemilia.

Rostra (speaker's platform)

Temple of Jupiter
The Capitoline Hill is where the great Temple of Jupiter stands. Jupiter is the most powerful Roman god.

Theater of Marcellus
This theater puts on the best plays in Rome. In the tragedies, people are killed, ghosts appear, and gods come down from the sky. Then the clowns rush on and give everyone a good laugh.

shopping complex

Senate house (Curia)

The great Augustus was Rome's first emperor. He built a new Forum, the Forum of Augustus, next to the Forum Romanum.

Titus's home

Titus's street

Viminal Hill

Quirinal Hill

Sublicius bridge

Emilian bridge

Basilica Aemilia

Basilica Julia

Fabrician bridge

Cestius bridge

Tiber River

Tiber island

Rome

In A.D. 128, Rome is at the center of the known world.

8

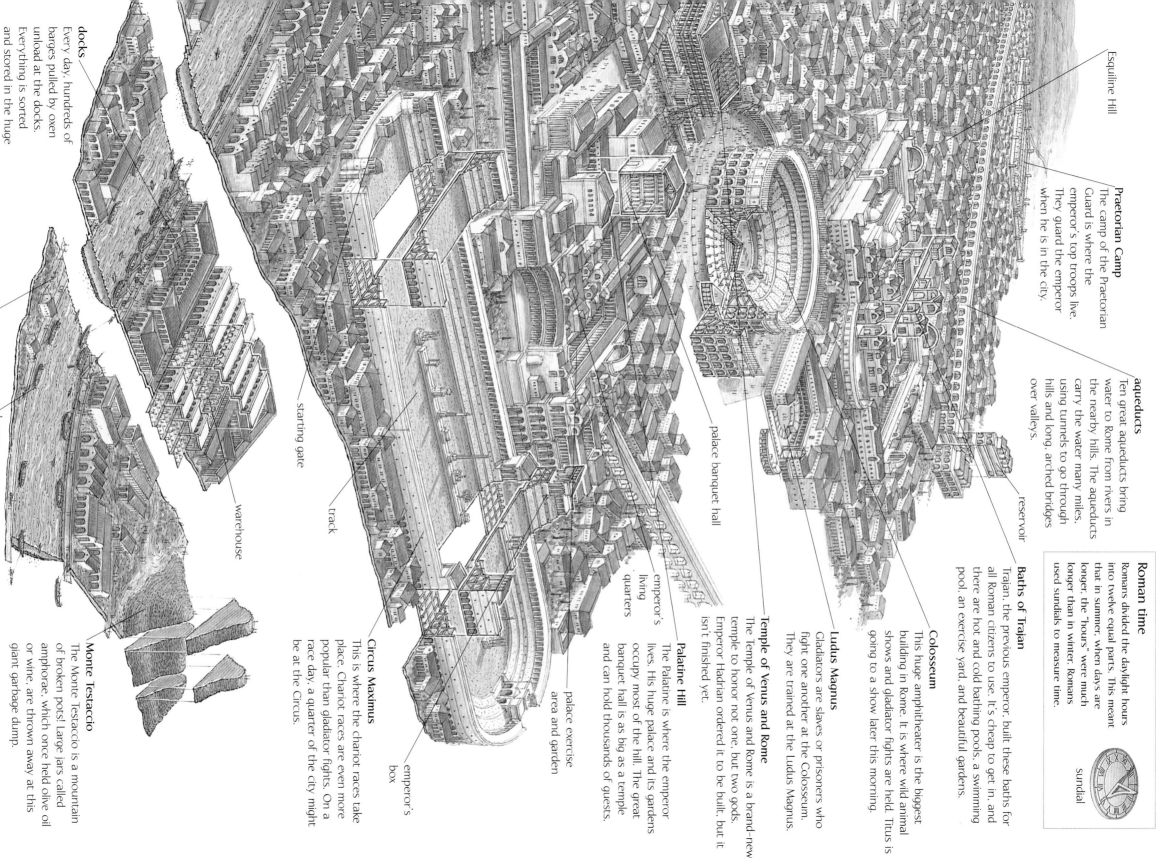

docks
Every day, hundreds of barges pulled by oxen unload at the docks. Everything is sorted and stored in the huge warehouses by the docks.

oxen

barge

warehouse

starting gate

track

Monte Testaccio
The Monte Testaccio is a mountain of broken pots! Large jars called amphorae, which once held olive oil or wine, are thrown away at this giant garbage dump.

Circus Maximus
This is where the chariot races take place. Chariot races are even more popular than gladiator fights. On a race day, a quarter of the city might be at the Circus.

emperor's box

palace exercise area and garden

emperor's living quarters

Palatine Hill
The Palatine is where the emperor lives. His huge palace and its gardens occupy most of the hill. The great banquet hall is as big as a temple and can hold thousands of guests.

Temple of Venus and Rome
The Temple of Venus and Rome is a brand-new temple to honor not one, but two gods. Emperor Hadrian ordered it to be built, but it isn't finished yet.

palace banquet hall

reservoir

aqueducts
Ten great aqueducts bring water to Rome from rivers in the nearby hills. The aqueducts carry the water many miles, using tunnels to go through hills and long, arched bridges over valleys.

Praetorian Camp
The camp of the Praetorian Guard is where the emperor's top troops live. They guard the emperor when he is in the city.

Esquiline Hill

Ludus Magnus
Gladiators are slaves or prisoners who fight one another at the Colosseum. They are trained at the Ludus Magnus.

Colosseum
This huge amphitheater is the biggest building in Rome. It is where wild animal shows and gladiator fights are held. Titus is going to a show later this morning.

Baths of Trajan
Trajan, the previous emperor, built these baths for all Roman citizens to use. It's cheap to get in, and there are hot and cold bathing pools, a swimming pool, an exercise yard, and beautiful gardens.

9

Titus's house

It's only just light, but at Titus's house everyone is busy. Because today is a festival day, Titus and his father will be out for the whole day, going to the Temple of Jupiter and visiting the games and the races. Titus's mother and baby sister stay at home. In the evening, the family is going to host a festival-day feast to celebrate.

atrium
The first room you come into is the atrium. This is a large hallway with a small pool in the center. There are stone carvings of Titus's ancestors around the atrium.

doorway
At night, the front door is guarded by a doorkeeper— a household slave with a guard dog. Titus and his family are rich, so they have many slaves. Slaves can be bought and sold at slave markets. They do most of the work around the house.

clients

water supply
Titus's family is lucky — they have a well in the house. Not many Roman houses have their own water supply.

bronzesmith's shop

shops
The two rooms that face the street are rented out as shops. The owners sleep above the shop at night. This morning they are already hard at work.

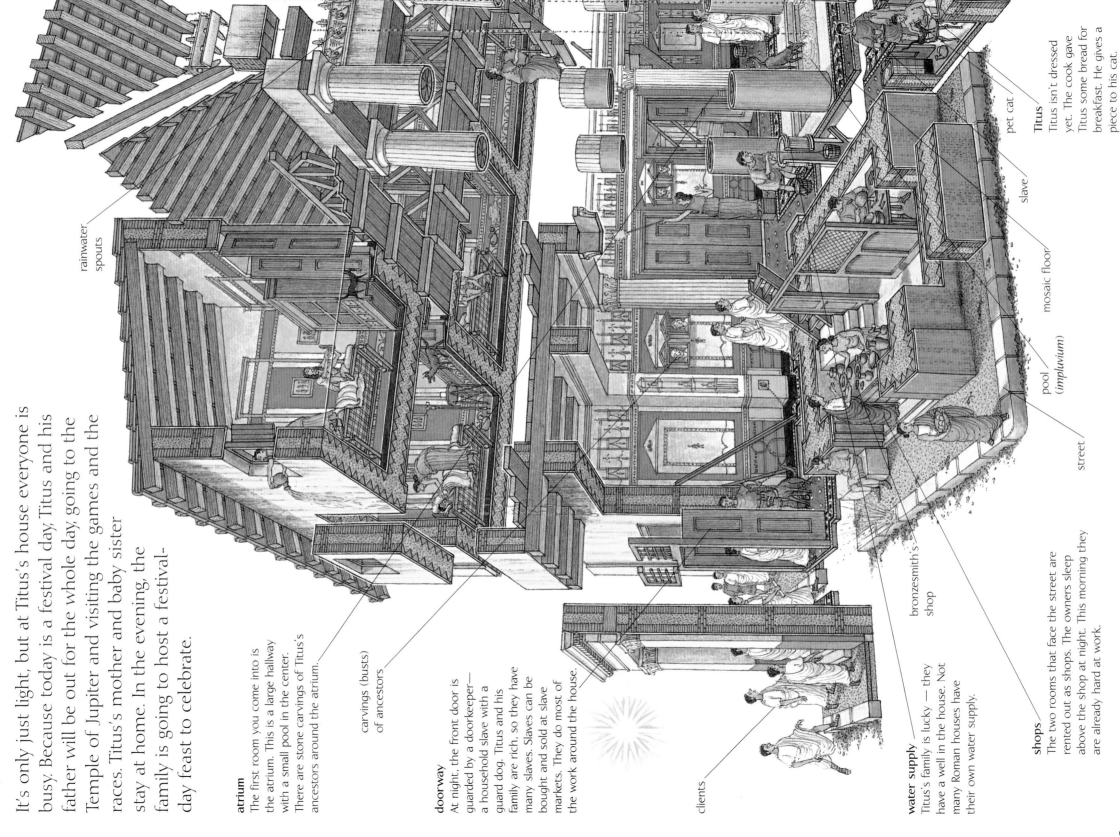

rainwater spouts

carvings (busts) of ancestors

pet cat

Titus
Titus isn't dressed yet. The cook gave Titus some bread for breakfast. He gives a piece to his cat.

slave

mosaic floor

pool (*impluvium*)

street

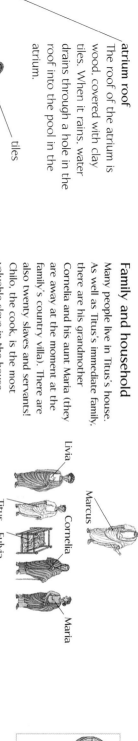

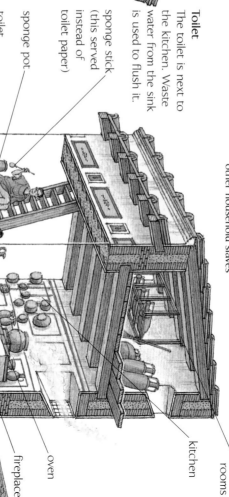

atrium roof
The roof of the atrium is wood, covered with clay tiles. When it rains, water drains through a hole in the roof into the pool in the atrium.

bedroom

baby Fulvia
Fulvia is Titus's new baby sister. Titus has two grown-up sisters, too, but they are married and don't live at home.

Marcus
Marcus, Titus's father, is seeing clients in the office. The clients are people who are less well-off than he. He helps them out, and sometimes finds them jobs. In return, they help him when there are elections.

dining room
The household slaves are cleaning the house for a dinner party tonight.

garden
Most of the vegetables and herbs for the house are grown in the garden. The covered walkway is cool in summer, but is warmed by the sun in winter.

shrine of the household gods (*lararium*)

Livia
Titus's mother Livia is in charge of the house, and will spend the day preparing for the dinner party. But before that, she has to burn incense on the household shrine (*lararium*) to honor the gods that guard the house and the pantry.

fireplace

oven

kitchen

slaves' rooms

Toilet
The toilet is next to the kitchen. Waste water from the sink is used to flush it.

sponge stick (this served instead of toilet paper)

sponge pot

toilet

drain

water fountain

Family and household
Many people live in Titus's house. As well as Titus's immediate family, there are his grandmother Cornelia and his aunt Maria (they are away at the moment at the family's country villa). There are also twenty slaves and servants! Chilo, the cook, is the most valuable slave in the house. His cooking is famous throughout Rome.

wooden roof beams

tiles

Livia's bedroom

Decimus (Marcus's secretary)

Nicander (Titus's tutor)

Livia

Cornelia

Marcus

Titus

Fulvia

Chilo (the cook)

Maria

Martilla (Livia's ornatrix, or hairdresser)

Potita (Fulvia's nanny)

slaves' other household slaves

During the 1st hour (6:30 A.M.)

In the street

Titus and his father set off for the Temple of Jupiter. On the way, they stop at the bakery near their home to talk to Hermes, the owner. Titus munches on a pizza while his father and Hermes talk business. Hermes is a freedman, or freed slave. He used to be the cook at Titus's house, but then he bought his freedom from Titus's father.

apartments
Most people in Rome live in high-rise apartment buildings like this. The first-floor apartments are large and roomy, but the top-floor apartments are tiny, single rooms with no water or cooking facilities.

During the 2nd hour (7:00 A.M.)

aqueduct bringing water from the hills

carts
Carts are banned from the narrow streets during the day, unless they are carrying building supplies. This one is bringing wood for a damaged building.

Titus's home

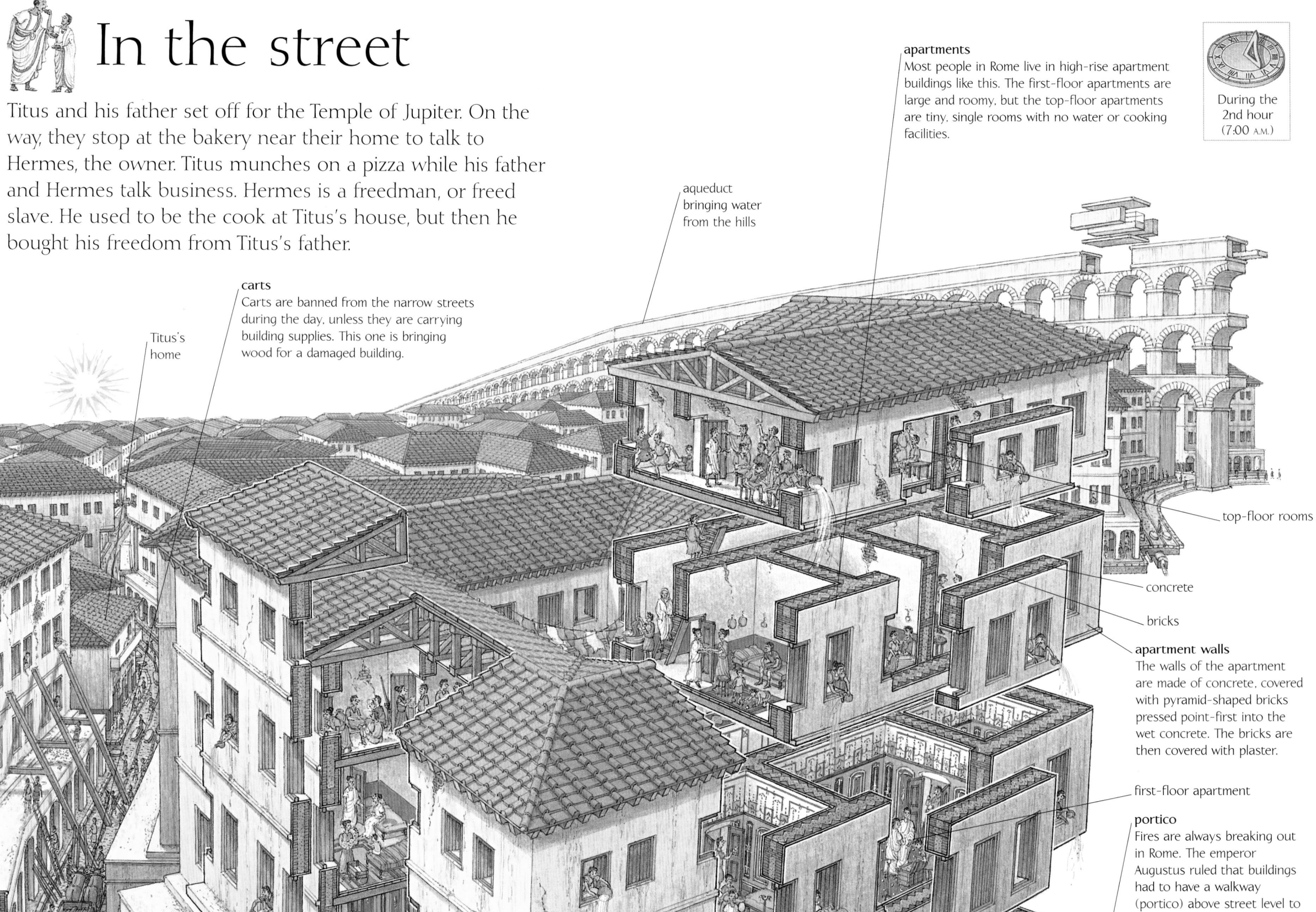

top-floor rooms

concrete

bricks

apartment walls
The walls of the apartment are made of concrete, covered with pyramid-shaped bricks pressed point-first into the wet concrete. The bricks are then covered with plaster.

first-floor apartment

portico
Fires are always breaking out in Rome. The emperor Augustus ruled that buildings had to have a walkway (portico) above street level to help firefighters get at fires.

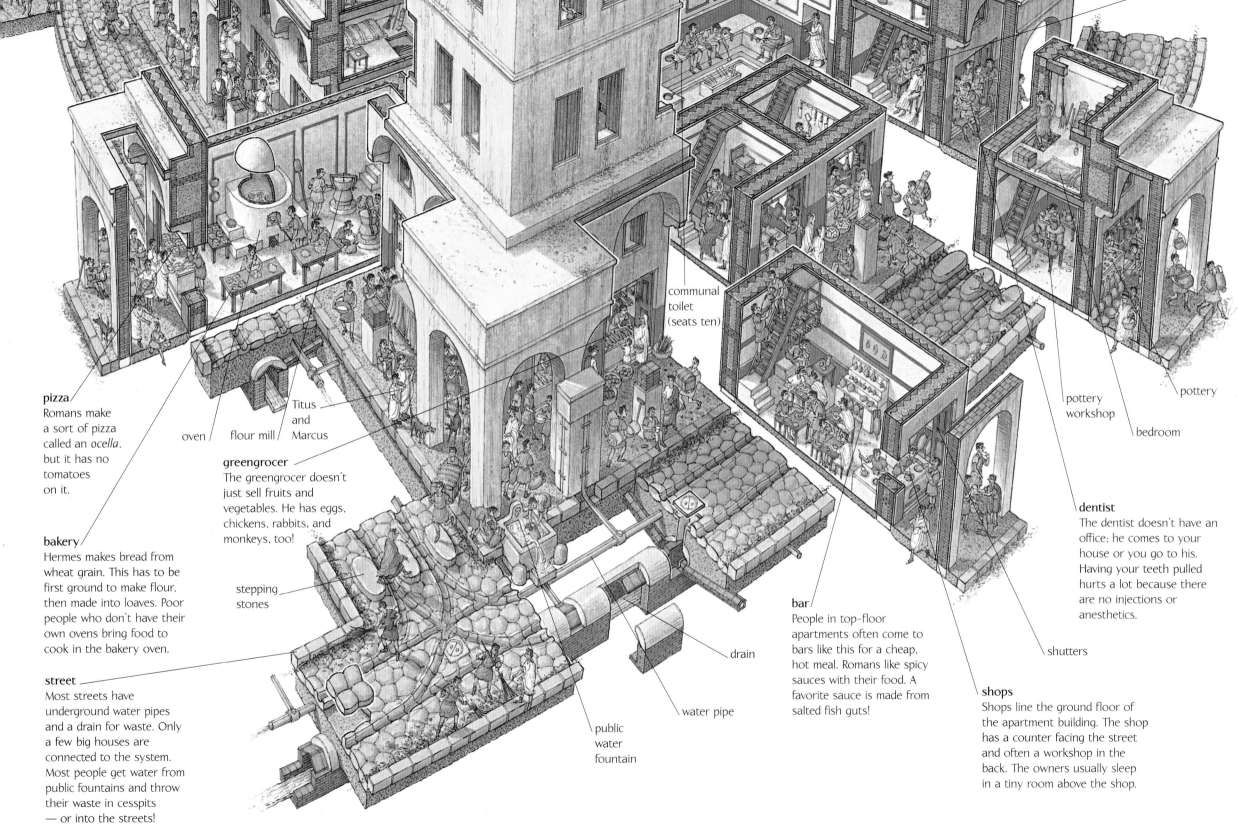

pizza
Romans make a sort of pizza called an *ocella*, but it has no tomatoes on it.

bakery
Hermes makes bread from wheat grain. This has to be first ground to make flour, then made into loaves. Poor people who don't have their own ovens bring food to cook in the bakery oven.

street
Most streets have underground water pipes and a drain for waste. Only a few big houses are connected to the system. Most people get water from public fountains and throw their waste in cesspits — or into the streets!

oven

flour mill

Titus and Marcus

greengrocer
The greengrocer doesn't just sell fruits and vegetables. He has eggs, chickens, rabbits, and monkeys, too!

stepping stones

public water fountain

water pipe

drain

communal toilet (seats ten)

bar
People in top-floor apartments often come to bars like this for a cheap, hot meal. Romans like spicy sauces with their food. A favorite sauce is made from salted fish guts!

shops
Shops line the ground floor of the apartment building. The shop has a counter facing the street and often a workshop in the back. The owners usually sleep in a tiny room above the shop.

pottery workshop

pottery

bedroom

dentist
The dentist doesn't have an office; he comes to your house or you go to his. Having your teeth pulled hurts a lot because there are no injections or anesthetics.

shutters

13

The Temple of Jupiter

There are lots of festival days each year, but Titus likes the festival of Castor and Pollux. Castor and Pollux are gods of horsemen, and so the parade includes hundreds of Roman cavalrymen. Titus loves watching the cavalrymen on their fine horses. They are wearing their best armor, and their shining bronze helmets and breastplates gleam in the sun. Titus and his father watch the horsemen pass, then join the parade.

The legend of Castor and Pollux
Hundreds of years ago, the Romans fought a battle against a group of enemies at Lake Regillus, southeast of Rome. The fight was going badly for the Romans until two shining young men named Castor and Pollux appeared on white horses and led them to victory. Later that day, the same men were seen watering their tired horses at a fountain in the Forum. They told the citizens about the victory at Lake Regillus and then disappeared. The temple of Castor and Pollux was built on the site of the fountain in the Forum.

During the
3rd hour
(8:10 A.M.)

Temple
The Temple itself is very beautiful. The columns are milky white marble, while the roof and doors are covered in gold. Inside there are huge gold and ivory statues of three gods: Jupiter, Juno, and Minerva.

The ceremony
At the start of the ceremony, the priest tosses incense into the altar flame and sprinkles wine and cakes on the altar. Next he offers up a prayer to Castor and Pollux. Now the animals are sacrificed. An official stuns each animal with a hammer, then another official kills it. Some of the meat from the sacrifices is burned on the altar fires. Afterward, the worshippers feast on the meat that is not burned.

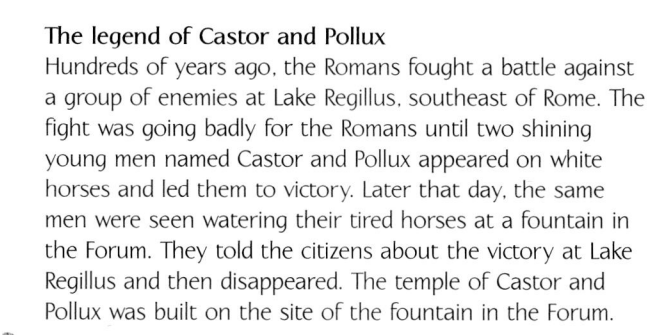

statue

carving of gods

statue

gold covering on tiles

bronze roof tiles

capital (top) of column

marble columns made of smaller drums

golden doors

Juno statue

marble drum

Minerva statue

Jupiter statue

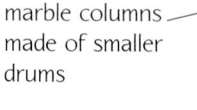

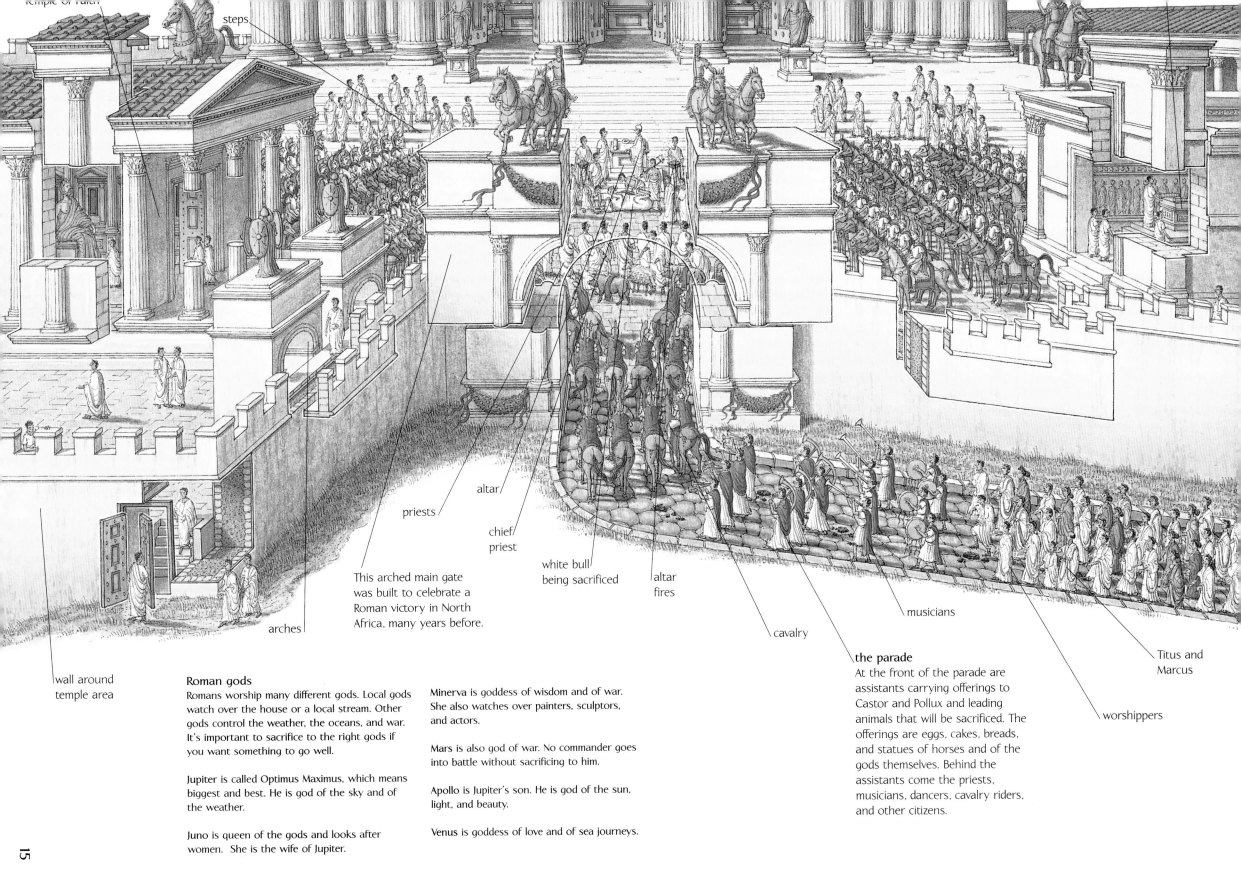

Temple of Faith

steps

priests

altar

chief
priest

white bull
being sacrificed

altar
fires

cavalry

musicians

This arched main gate
was built to celebrate a
Roman victory in North
Africa, many years before.

arches

wall around
temple area

worshippers

Titus and
Marcus

the parade
At the front of the parade are
assistants carrying offerings to
Castor and Pollux and leading
animals that will be sacrificed. The
offerings are eggs, cakes, breads,
and statues of horses and of the
gods themselves. Behind the
assistants come the priests,
musicians, dancers, cavalry riders,
and other citizens.

Roman gods
Romans worship many different gods. Local gods
watch over the house or a local stream. Other
gods control the weather, the oceans, and war.
It's important to sacrifice to the right gods if
you want something to go well.

Jupiter is called Optimus Maximus, which means
biggest and best. He is god of the sky and of
the weather.

Juno is queen of the gods and looks after
women. She is the wife of Jupiter.

Minerva is goddess of wisdom and of war.
She also watches over painters, sculptors,
and actors.

Mars is also god of war. No commander goes
into battle without sacrificing to him.

Apollo is Jupiter's son. He is god of the sun,
light, and beauty.

Venus is goddess of love and of sea journeys.

15

The Forum Romanum

After the parade, Titus and his father head for the games at the Colosseum. On their way through the Forum Romanum, they meet another senator, named Antony. Marcus and Antony run a business together, bringing olive oil from Spain to Rome. Antony says that a ship has just arrived with a new cargo of olive oil. "I'll go to the docks later to check the cargo," says Marcus.

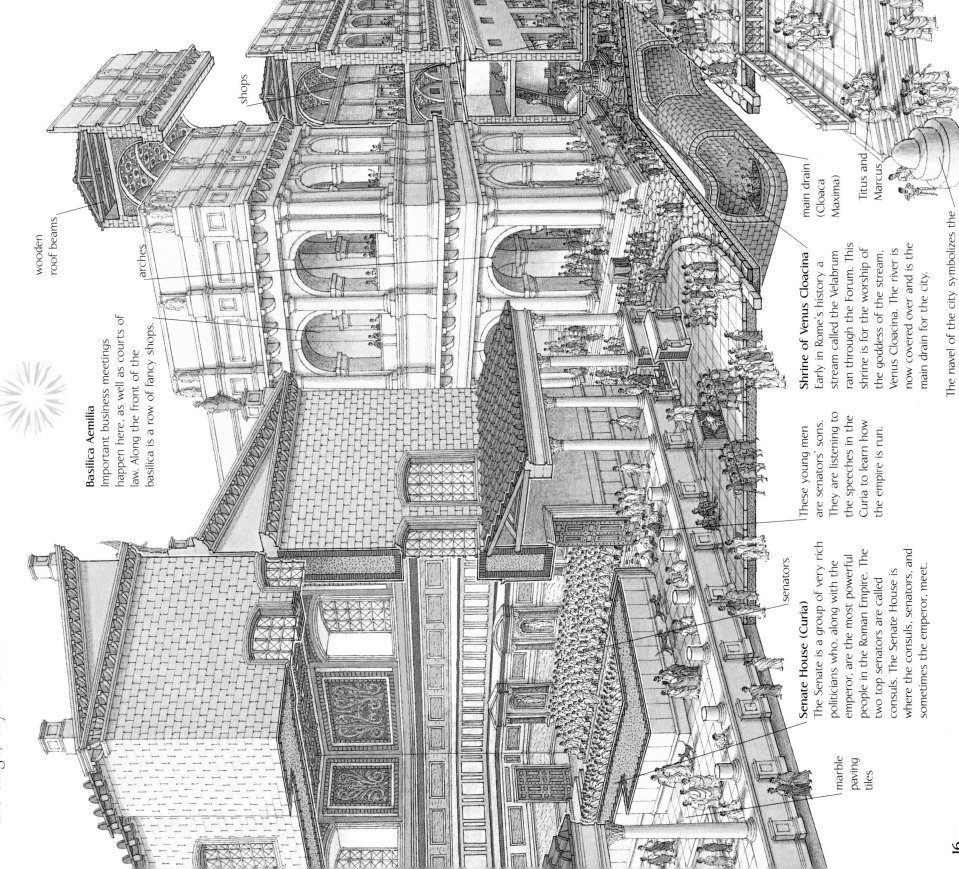

wooden roof beams

shops

arches

Basilica Aemilia
Important business meetings happen here, as well as courts of law. Along the front of the basilica is a row of fancy shops.

senators

Senate House (Curia)
The Senate is a group of very rich politicians who, along with the emperor, are the most powerful people in the Roman Empire. The two top senators are called consuls. The Senate House is where the consuls, senators, and sometimes the emperor, meet.

These young men are senators' sons. They are listening to the speeches in the Curia to learn how the empire is run.

marble paving tiles

Shrine of Venus Cloacina
Early in Rome's history a stream called the Velabrum ran through the Forum. This shrine is for the worship of the goddess of the stream, Venus Cloacina. The river is now covered over and is the main drain for the city.

The navel of the city symbolizes the center of the city and the Roman world.

main drain (Cloaca Maxima)

Titus and Marcus.

16

Citizens, Freedmen, and slaves

Everyone in Italy who is born free (not a slave) is a Roman citizen. This means that they can vote for government officials when there are elections.

The emperor is the most important citizen. The first emperor, Augustus, called himself "first among equals."

The consuls and senators are next in importance. They are all very rich and powerful.

The knights (equites) are rich citizens who have important jobs in the army and the government.

Ordinary citizens are much poorer than senators or knights. Many are shopkeepers or farmers.

Freedmen and women are freed slaves. They often become shopkeepers, too.

Slaves are mostly foreign prisoners who are bought and sold. Some have terrible jobs such as working in mines. But a few skilled slaves, such as actors or cooks, become rich and famous.

Temple of Vesta

Vesta is the goddess of the hearth (home fire). Inside the Temple of Vesta is a holy fire, which is the "hearth" for the whole city. The fire is kept alive day and night by a group of priestesses called the Vestal Virgins.

Temple of Divus Julius

When the Roman leader Julius Caesar was killed, this temple was built in his honor. People began to worship him like a god. Augustus and other emperors who have died have temples and are worshipped as gods, too.

Temple of Castor and Pollux

The Temple of Castor and Pollux is decorated in honor of the day's festival. The temple is a center for banking and also the office of weights and measures.

Arch of Augustus

This arch was built by the Emperor Augustus to celebrate his victories in battle.

peg holes

pegs

ships' prows

The golden milestone shows the distances to all key cities in the Roman Empire.

speaker's platform

This Rostra is a platform for public speeches. Around the edges are the prows (fronts) of warships that the Romans captured in battle.

Important people sometimes travel in litters like this one.

People scratch game boards on these steps to play checkers and dice games.

Forum

The Forum is the center of Rome. This is where the Empire is governed and where the laws are made.

nave

galleries

Basilica Julia

Some of Rome's most important courts of law are held in the Basilica Julia and in the Basilica Aemilia (opposite). The high space in the center of the basilica is called the nave. Around it are galleries on two stories.

During the 4th hour (10:15 A.M.)

17

The Colosseum

Titus is really looking forward to the games; he hasn't been to the Colosseum before. It's early, but the amphitheater is already filled with a roaring crowd of thousands of people. The show starts with some amazing performing elephants. One draws letters in the sand with its foot. Next, the hunters enter, each carrying only a spear. Snarling lions and leopards appear from nowhere and surround the hunters. The big cats attack.

Colossus

The Colossus gives the Colosseum its name. It is a statue of the sun god, Helios, and is about 100 feet tall.

construction

Seven rings of pillars hold up the Colosseum, with 80 pillars in each ring. More than half a million tons of stone were used in the lower levels of the building.

entrances

There are 76 public entrances to the Colosseum. It is free to enter, but you must have a numbered ticket. The number tells you which entrance you must use.

Gladiators

Gladiators are criminals, slaves, or prisoners captured in war. Pairs of gladiators are forced to fight to the death. The *hoplomachus* and the *secutor* are heavily armed gladiators. They each have a helmet, a large shield, and a straight sword. The Thracian and the *retiarius* are more lightly armed. Lightest armed of all are the *venatores*, or wild-animal hunters. They have no shields and are armed only with spears.

concrete and brick
The upper parts of the building are made of brick and concrete. Roman concrete is waterproof and strengthens with age.

vomitoria
There are 64 entrances (*vomitoria*) to the seating area. This means that if there is a fire or an emergency, everyone can get out quickly.

sand

animal cages
Wild animals are held in these cages before they go into the arena.

stone posts
to anchor the awning ropes to the masts

hoplomachus Thracian *retiarius* *secutor* *venatores*

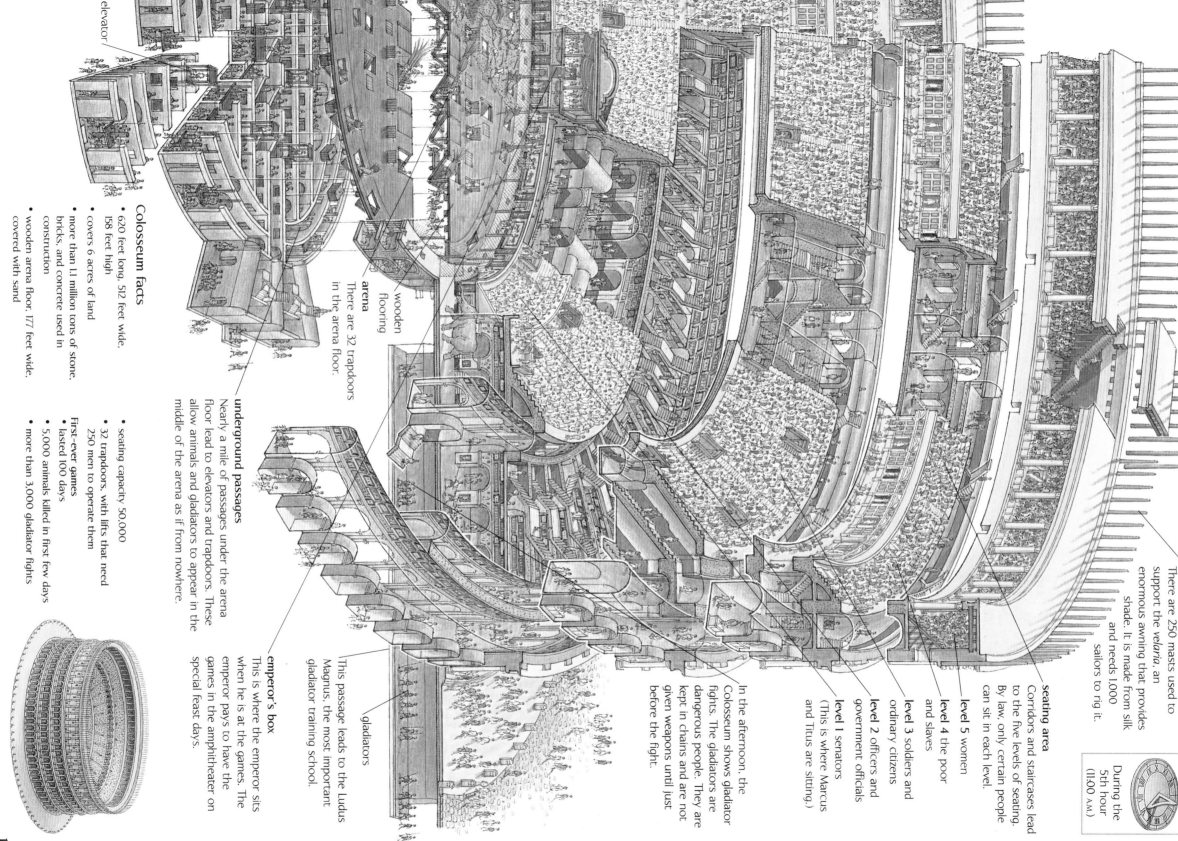

elevator

wooden
flooring

arena
There are 32 trapdoors
in the arena floor.

Colosseum facts

- 620 feet long, 512 feet wide,
  158 feet high
- covers 6 acres of land
- more than 1.1 million tons of stone,
  bricks, and concrete used in
  construction
- wooden arena floor, 177 feet wide,
  covered with sand

- seating capacity 50,000
- 32 trapdoors, with lifts that need
  250 men to operate them

First-ever games
- lasted 100 days
- 5,000 animals killed in first few days
- more than 3,000 gladiator fights

underground passages
Nearly a mile of passages under the arena
floor lead to elevators and trapdoors. These
allow animals and gladiators to appear in the
middle of the arena as if from nowhere.

emperor's box
This is where the emperor sits
when he is at the games. The
emperor pays to have the
games in the amphitheater on
special feast days.

gladiators
This passage leads to the Ludus
Magnus, the most important
gladiator training school.

In the afternoon, the
Colosseum shows gladiator
fights. The gladiators are
dangerous people. They are
kept in chains and are not
given weapons until just
before the fight.

masts
There are 250 masts used to
support the *velaria*, an
enormous awning that provides
shade. It is made from silk
and needs 1,000
sailors to rig it.

seating area
Corridors and staircases lead
to the five levels of seating.
By law, only certain people
can sit in each level.

level 5 women

level 4 the poor
and slaves

level 3 soldiers and
ordinary citizens

level 2 officers and
government officials

level 1 senators
(This is where Marcus
and Titus are sitting.)

During the
5th hour
(11:00 A.M.)

19

At the docks

During the
7th hour
(2:30 P.M.)

Titus's father has to go to the docks to check on his cargo of olive oil. Everyone at the docks is incredibly busy. Crane ropes creak, oxen bellow, and the air smells of wine, olives, and sweaty bodies. Grumpy porters yell and jostle anyone who gets in their way. *Oof!* One of them bashes into Titus.

Titus's father talks to an official about his cargo. They go to make sure that the oil is good quality.

Goods from around the world

A city of more than a million people eats a lot! Every day, merchants bring in many tons of food and other goods from all over the known world. There is wheat, building stone, and papyrus from Egypt; wine from Greece and Gaul (France); wool, pottery, and perfumes from Syria and Arabia; wood and horses from Dacia (Eastern Europe); wild animals from North Africa; gold, copper, oil, and wine from Spain; and wool, tin, and iron from Britannia (Britain).

Large ships bringing food and other cargo cannot get up the Tiber River, so they unload at the port of Ostia on the coast. The ship's cargo is then loaded onto barges and pulled up the river by teams of oxen.

Monte Testaccio ("hill of pots")
This hill is about 100 feet high, taller than four houses, and it's made entirely of broken pots! Used olive oil amphoras are dumped here because they become smelly and can't be used again. Walls divide each level of the hill into small areas to stop the whole thing from collapsing. The pots are covered with lime to keep them from smelling.

← To Ostia

Tiber River

empty barges returning to Ostia

team of oxen

towpath

donkeys carrying amphoras

vaulted (arched) ceiling

shelving for amphoras

sacks of grain

wool

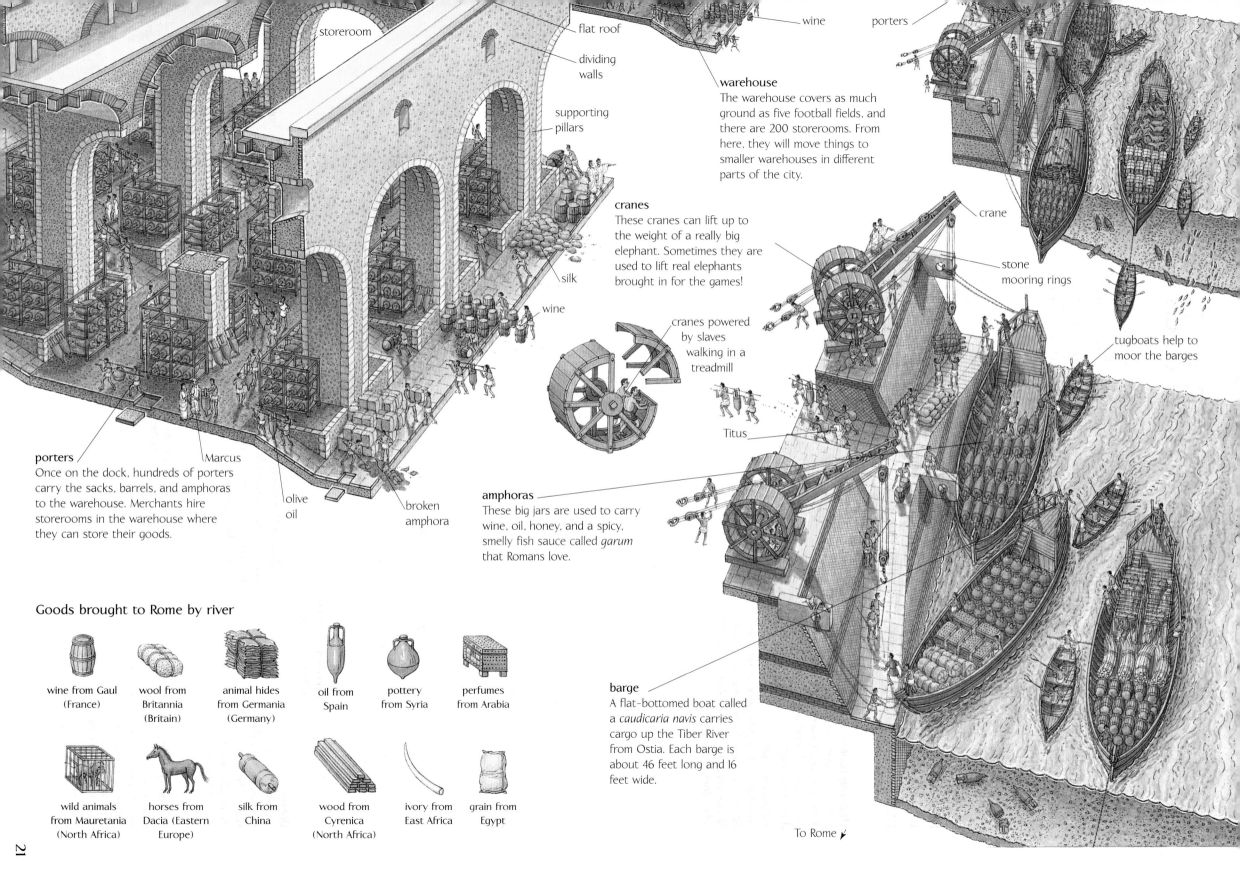

storeroom

flat roof

dividing walls

supporting pillars

silk

wine

olive oil

broken amphora

wine

porters

warehouse
The warehouse covers as much ground as five football fields, and there are 200 storerooms. From here, they will move things to smaller warehouses in different parts of the city.

cranes
These cranes can lift up to the weight of a really big elephant. Sometimes they are used to lift real elephants brought in for the games!

cranes powered by slaves walking in a treadmill

Titus

crane

stone mooring rings

tugboats help to moor the barges

porters
Once on the dock, hundreds of porters carry the sacks, barrels, and amphoras to the warehouse. Merchants hire storerooms in the warehouse where they can store their goods.

Marcus

amphoras
These big jars are used to carry wine, oil, honey, and a spicy, smelly fish sauce called *garum* that Romans love.

Goods brought to Rome by river

wine from Gaul (France)

wool from Britannia (Britain)

animal hides from Germania (Germany)

oil from Spain

pottery from Syria

perfumes from Arabia

wild animals from Mauretania (North Africa)

horses from Dacia (Eastern Europe)

silk from China

wood from Cyrenica (North Africa)

ivory from East Africa

grain from Egypt

barge
A flat-bottomed boat called a *caudicaria navis* carries cargo up the Tiber River from Ostia. Each barge is about 46 feet long and 16 feet wide.

To Rome ↙

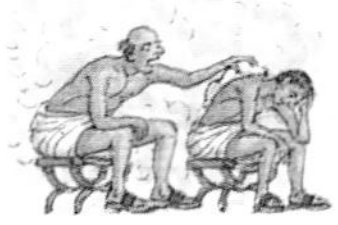

The Baths of Trajan

After the dock visit, Titus and his father go to relax and wash at the baths. They meet lots of friends there. Titus swims while his father plays ball and has a massage. Then they soak in the hot tub before taking a refreshing plunge in the cold pool. Titus's father buys them both a drink before they leave.

All Romans enjoy coming to the baths. It is not just a place to wash. People exercise, have a massage, talk business, have a bite to eat, go for a walk, read, or just relax and chat with friends. Women and men usually bathe at different times, women in the morning and men in the mid-afternoon.

Changing rooms
In the changing rooms (not shown here), there are open lockers where you can leave your clothes. People pay a slave to look after their belongings.

swimming pool
Swimming is a popular way to exercise. Before the public baths were built, many Romans kept fit by swimming across the Tiber River every day.

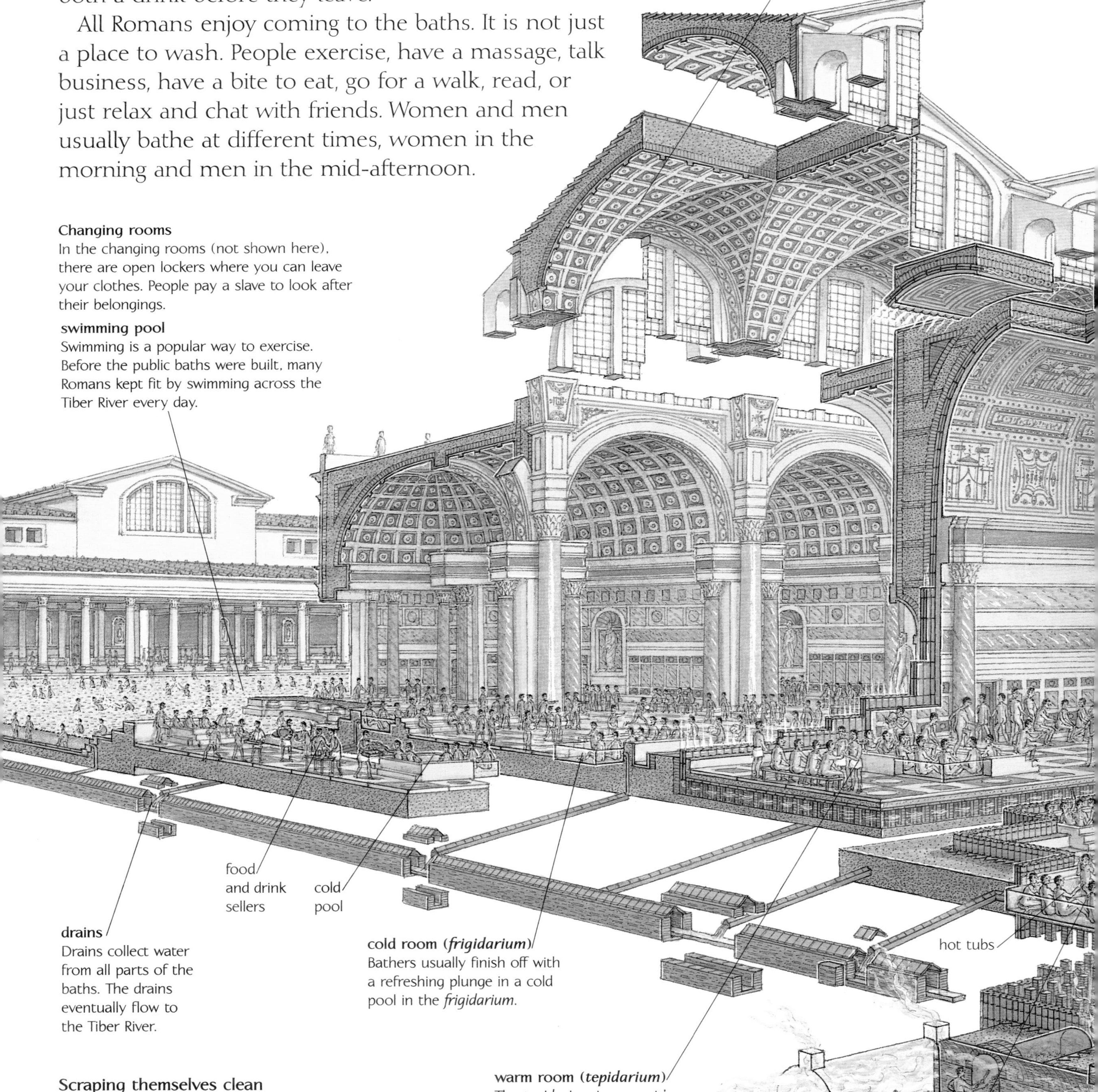

drains
Drains collect water from all parts of the baths. The drains eventually flow to the Tiber River.

Scraping themselves clean
Romans don't wash with soap. First, they exercise or sunbathe to get themselves sweaty. Then they get a slave attendant to rub their skin with oil. Finally, the slave scrapes off the oil and dirt using a scraper called a strigil.

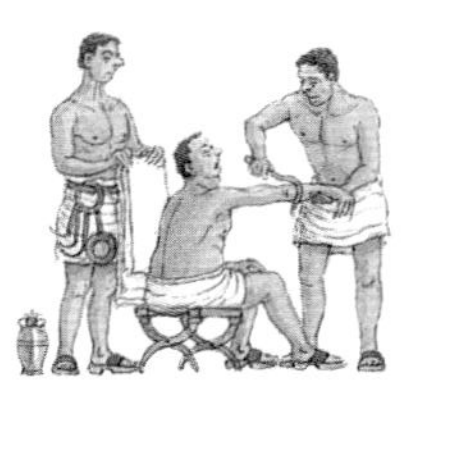

ceiling
The vaulted (arched) ceiling is made of concrete. The square decorations are called coffers, and they help give the ceiling strength.

hot tubs

hot room (*caldarium*)
People start to relax by relaxing in steaming hot water tubs in the hot room (*caldarium*).

warm room (*tepidarium*)
The *tepidarium* is warm; it's a place to cool off a little after the *caldarium*.

cold room (*frigidarium*)
Bathers usually finish off with a refreshing plunge in a cold pool in the *frigidarium*.

food and drink sellers

cold pool

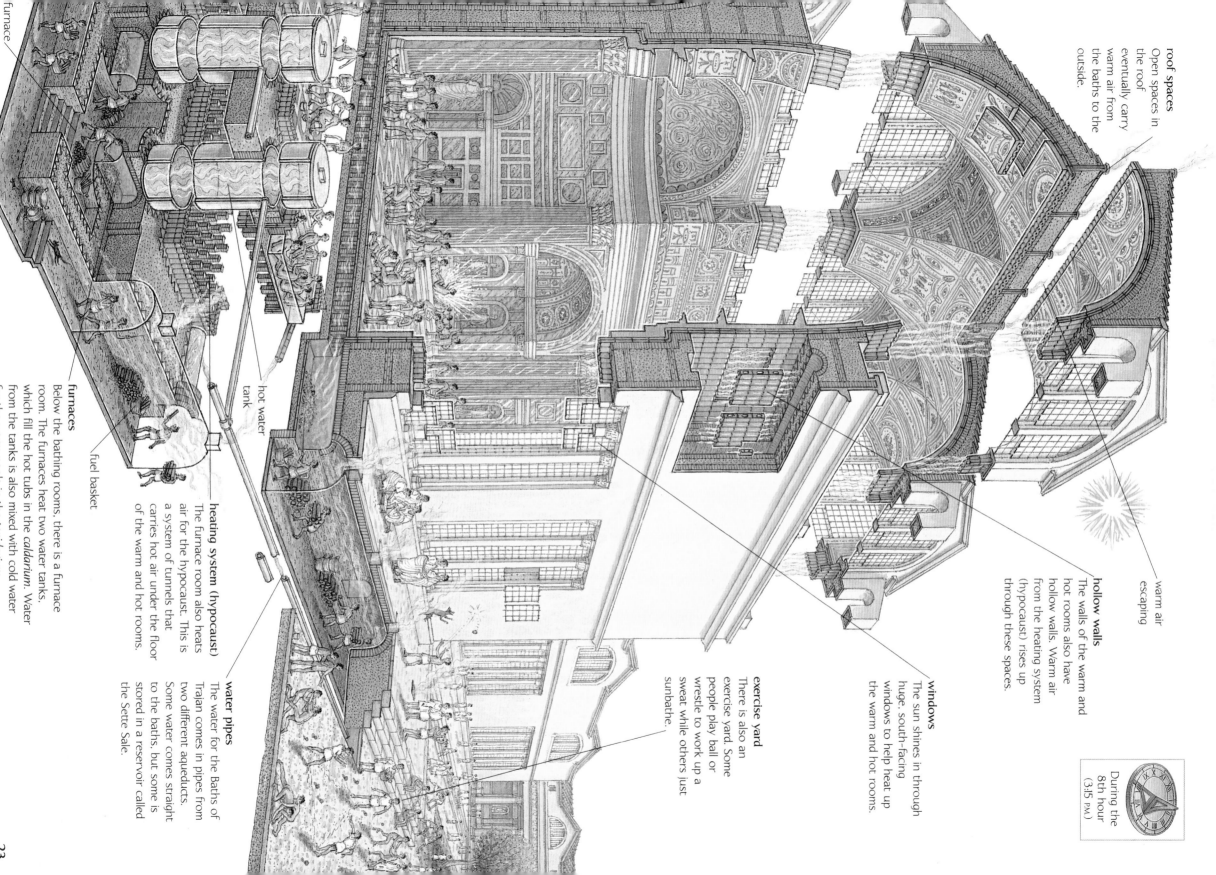

roof spaces
Open spaces in the roof eventually carry warm air from the baths to the outside.

warm air escaping

hollow walls
The walls of the warm and hot rooms also have hollow walls. Warm air from the heating system (hypocaust) rises up through these spaces.

windows
The sun shines in through huge, south-facing windows to help heat up the warm and hot rooms.

exercise yard
There is also an exercise yard. Some people play ball or wrestle to work up a sweat while others just sunbathe.

water pipes
The water for the Baths of Trajan comes in pipes from two different aqueducts. Some water comes straight to the baths, but some is stored in a reservoir called the Sette Sale.

heating system (hypocaust)
The furnace room also heats air for the hypocaust. This is a system of tunnels that carries hot air under the floor of the warm and hot rooms.

furnaces
Below the bathing rooms, there is a furnace room. The furnaces heat two water tanks, which fill the hot tubs in the caldarium. Water from the tanks is also mixed with cold water for the warm pools in the tepidarium.

fuel basket

hot water tank

furnace room

23

At the races

The best treat of the day is the chariot races at the Circus Maximus. Everyone is shouting for their favorite team. Titus and his father support the Green team. "Come on Greens!" Titus yells. But on the first turn, a Red charioteer swings around too tightly and his chariot turns over – right in the path of one of the Green chariots. Luckily, the drivers are unhurt. They struggle to cut their horses free before the other chariots come around again.

Circus Maximus

The Circus Maximus is the biggest stadium ever! It is nearly 2,000 feet long – bigger than any modern sports stadium. It holds 250,000 people. The Circus was first laid out by Rome's King Tarquin, in about 500 B.C.

spina

The *spina* runs down the middle of the circus like the guardrail on a highway. Three pillars at either end mark the turning points.

chariot teams

Each chariot and charioteer belongs to one of four teams: Reds, Whites, Greens, or Blues. There are twelve chariots in the race, three from each team. These chariots are *quadrigas* (four-horse teams).

betting

All through the crowd, people are betting on who will win the race. Roman law says that betting is illegal, but no one seems to mind!

water pools

Each team has a water pool on the *spina*. As their chariots go past, slaves throw water on the sweating horses.

starting gates

The starting gates have separate boxes for each chariot. A trumpet sounds to start the race. A clever mechanism makes all twelve gates spring open at once, and the chariots charge out.

dolphin statues

spring-operated starting gates

starting boxes

snack seller

Titus and Marcus

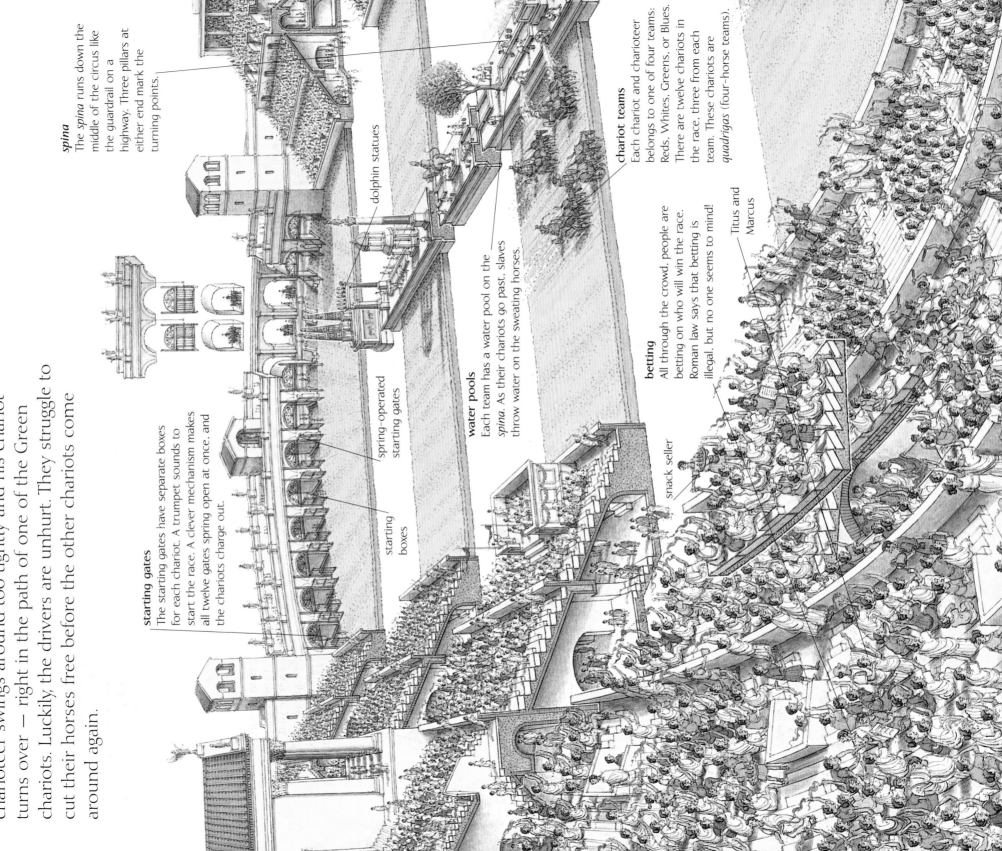